Living Life With Accountability

Choices to Decisions

Publisher: Endless Road Publishing
Denver, Colorado
United States of America

LIBRARY OF CONGRESS CONTROL NUMBER:
ISBN:1475133642

EAN-13:9781475133646

Printed in the United States of America by CreateSpac e
Bulk purchases, please contact the author

Your Change, Your Challenge

Whether your change challenge is a career, a job, no job, an unhappy work/life balance, these pages are for you. My goal is to help you to refocus your efforts to better understand what is today and where tomorrow can be. Navigate your journey with action tasks that guide you to and through the obstructions you will encounter along your way.

GPS For Your Life Navigation

1. Identify where you are
2. Locate which direction to go
3. Create the map
4. Select navigation support people and tools
5. Start
6. Take notes and assess your travel
7. Go back to Step 1

Locate ideas that can help you wherever you are in your very own journey

Richard Oppenheim
Your GPS Navigator

STUCK IS NOT A GOOD PLACE TO BE

Being stuck is unhealthy
Being stuck is depressing
Being stuck is wrong

NASA's Spirit Rover got stuck in the sand on Mars. All the engineers and all the scientists could not get the stuck robot to move out of its stuck place.

The distance between Mars and Earth varies from 36 million miles (nearest planet after Venus) to over 250 million miles. That is a long distance to get something unstuck. What is the distance between where you are and where you want to be?

What does it take for you to get unstuck?

- Wash off sand?
- Dry up the mud?
- Work for NASA?
- Recognize what is causing your being stuck?
- Willingness to be unstuck and to get going?
- Desire to be unstuck and to get going?
- Courage to be unstuck and to get going?

Sometimes, getting unstuck can benefit from:

- A push from family, friends, associates, strangers
- A push from a plow or tow truck
- Help from a mentor
- Guidance and encouragement from a coach

Does what you are doing make sense?

- Are you in the right company?
- Is your location satisfying?
- How are you dealing with family?
- Did your football team make the right draft choices?

Sense is that word we use to determine whether we agree with what just happened, did happen or will happen in the future. There are many things throughout our lives that can make sense along with a large number of things that make no sense at all. For example: traffic jams, a team losing the game, not getting the promotion, getting the promotion, the price of food, an argument, and many, many more.

The ability to sense what is happening as it is happening is a valuable skill. This skill is not part of your birthing DNA; it develops over a long time period. Moreover, it is something that you need to keep learning, modifying, and letting go of what was. Jane Austen's book, "Sense and Sensibility" is only one example of how people view good sense, bad sense and nonsense.

Using your senses is an all the time activity. Updating and upgrading your use of senses needs to be a constant throughout your long life. Your senses will help you to keep moving ahead. Getting stuck never makes good sense. When you pay attention to your senses, you can assess the good and bad of any action.

THINGS TO DO TO GET YOU UP AND GOING

Establish a Goal

Do not overthink the goal setting. Make it something that you already know needs to be accomplished in the the next 90 days.

- Goals include: play time, work time, family time, and combinations

- Write the goals as reminders to keep you focused

- The goals need not be what you want to get done, not your forever dream

- Examples: connect with a friend, buy a birthday gift, watch a movie, finish writing the white paper or book, start a blog, etc

Plan

Complicated plans need strategies, tactics, budgets, people, project schedule, etc. A 3 month plan needs less than a single page.

- Make it easy for you to measure when successful

- Be concise and clear enough you can share these plans in 2 minutes

- Review the economics and be sure that any cash needed is available without debt

- Share the plan with others to make sure you understand what is to be done

- Set up a schedule for each task to be completed - avoid too much detail

Now do it.

Don't wait around for the right time or the right opportunity. There never will be a right time or right opportunity. Just get going.

The infamous To Do list is not impossible. Here is my 4 step plan.

1. **List all To Be Done tasks**

2. **Pick any two of them**

3. **Do the selected two**

4. **Go back to step 1**

Get Going

Making your way in the world requires a destination, a map and a compass in that order.
Before any journey begins, you must establish a destination. Of course, any destination includes a direction.

Say you want to go for a drive and do not have a particular stopping point determined. I have done this often throughout my life. It started with my Schwinn bicycle that had fat tires and two speeds - forward and stop. Cars were easier, faster and carried passengers. They also cost more.

Picking a destination is a required part of your journey. Understand that the destination does not have to be as precise as exact latitude and longitude. If I want to drive from Denver to Las Vegas there are alternative routes with different terrains and different potential obstructions.

So pick a destination. If help is needed ask a friend a co-worker, a family member, someone you have not talked with for a long time.

Now is the best time to start going.

Seeking all the answers as to why one thing or another is happening, delays getting things done. Answers should be sought and remembered. Finding 'all' will not happen. You will locate information to keep going or stop.

One of the problems today is that very good people are part of the over qualified and over experienced looking for any job that can deliver a paycheck. Too many people must reinvent and reengineer what they say to make them more employable. It is not lies that are being proposed. It is the essential focus on what the needs are and how people can fit together. It is a shame that people have to mask some of what they are to be able to get a job.

Full employment will never happen. My prayers are that the anger and frustration felt by those without a job will not merge with the anger and frustration of people who are employed but doing 2-3 times the amount of work to make up for the folks who have been laid off. Anger and frustration is such a volatile mix of emotions that we cannot plan for the potential threat that it represents.

It is essential to maintain cool with the folks that are angry and frustrated. They need a kind word, a compliment, friendship during this turmoil in their lives. They do not benefit from any comment that states "Things will be alright" or "God has a plan for you" or "You are just not trying hard enough." Those phrases are patronizing and not helpful for people who need encouragement and support, not sympathy.

You Have Choices

Making decisions is never about choosing between right and wrong. It is about making choices that fit your journey that extends from where you are to where you want to be. When you look, you may first discover no choices ahead. This indicates you are looking in the wrong place or seeking the wrong things. When you want to fill up your car with gas, going to a library will not produce results.

When you have discovered choices, now you are faced with the opportunity to select one. Go to a restaurant and they have a bunch of items from which you can choose. There is the often heard cry – "I cannot make up my mind." Yes you can, just dig down and stop analyzing and pick. Sometimes the food choice will be great sometimes less than great. Picking does not always guarantee wonderful results. Picking means you get to move along with table conversation, finishing eating so you can get to your appointment on time, and so on.

Does a choice have to be made?

When driving anywhere, there are lots of choices - avoid other cars, traffic light signals, stop signs, directional turns, speed limits and so much more. If you want dinner before the restaurant closes, you have to make a selection. Know that many choices can be made without lots of contemplation, worry and any sense of feeling bad about choosing incorrectly. Of course, when the choices are about life risk actions - surgery, marriage, moving away to a new location – time to ponder is valuable.

Do you have sufficient facts, resources and information?

It would be wonderful if we can be assured that we always have 100 % of all the information about all of the choices to be made. Sometimes we do, most of the time we do not. Making the choice is based on our experiences - driving to a friend's house, answering a child's question, selecting the wine to accompany dinner, etc. Risk is often defined as making a decision when not all the facts are known.

How you make choices and decisions will say a lot about how you combine knowledge, experience, research, confidence and courage. You made it to where you are making lots of choices. Go ahead and make the next one and the one after that.

Will you take full responsibility for the outcome(s)?

Is the choice for you alone, just your friend, your spouse, your family, the department or the entire organization? Confidence and courage are required for any of these choices. The more people that are affected should lead you to engage with others before the choices are made.

The person responsible for your actions or inactions will be the primary guide for your moving forward. Do not duck and hide from taking responsibility. The consequences of NOT taking responsibility are far worse than lying. The key is to unlock your courage and stand up for your actions and who you are. When you do, the path to making decisions in your life gets better.

Do you understand the issues surrounding the situation?

Assume is one of those words that need to be moderated. Making assumptions does not have just one set of guidelines. There has to be a gathering of assumptions within the context of your current choice requirements. Traveling to the Moon, or beyond, cannot rely on assumptions about weather, solar winds, other objects, approximately where the moon's orbit will be in the next week and so on. Specifics are required.

On the other hand, business decisions combine facts with assumptions. One can anticipate what the economy will be next year. Assumptions made for next year always include some amount of risk surrounding the unknown. This risk analysis requires making choices from the range of variables that can occur.

Do you seek help?

No one knows everything. Sometimes it feels like that, but no there are gaps in everyone's ability to know the facts and then do an analysis of what is known and what is unknown. As a writer, I will never outgrow my need for good editors. Mistakes, misuse of words, lack of clarity and typing errors are best located and corrected prior to publication.

When you choose to seek assistance, it does not mean that you are deficient in any way. In business and your life, help is something that should be sought. Offering help to others is always a good choice.

Do you like your choices?

This can be a tough question. First, we may not know the outcome of our choice for a while. My second marriage was and still is a very good choice. I have no expectation that that good feeling will change. There are choices that we all have made that we wish we did not. This self-judgment for things that you did typically often eliminates the facts surrounding why the choice was made at that time. What you are most annoyed with is the outcome of that choice. Never underestimate the unknowns that follow every choice.

Never fear making the next choice, just because a prior choice was incorrect. Life is a never-ending series of choices, decision, choices, decisions and choices to be made based on prior decisions. What is worse is not making a choice and/or allowing someone else to make the choice for you. Stand up four own ability to make choices then work very hard to make the outcomes of each choice successful.

THE CHALLENGE OF CHOICE

How do your choices get made?

- Do you flip a coin and wait until the coin shows heads?
- Do you close your eyes and let randomness place your finger on the selection?
- Do you analyze possibilities with little or lots of time?
- Do you only continue whatever you did before?
- Do you wait for someone to make decisions for you?

The opportunity for choice ranges from auto-response to careful consideration to making no choice (which is a decision by you). Pulling your hand away from a hot stove should be automatic. Where to live will take more than just an instant muscle reflex.

The opportunity to choose requires us to be active in the decision process. The choice may have a significant impact on your life (marriage, children, career) or the choice could be simple (saying 'thank you', helping a friend, being kind). Whatever the range of choices, you have to be a participant in the process. Frequently, choices are a result of group interaction.

The challenges of climbing Mt Everest, swimming with a Great White Shark, or running a sub-4 minute mile are not part of this discussion. Those are very real challenges that will be attempted by a very few. You have choices that do not include the risk of putting your life in danger. Yes, going out in the world has a risk - tripping on the sidewalk, eating bad food, or the often quoted getting hit by a bus.

Choices appear frequently throughout every day. These choices will vary depending upon your circumstance. For example, if you are reading this you have access to a computer and the internet. Many do not. Most of us can choose food based on what we can afford and what we like. Many in the world have no such choice.

The value of making choices cannot be understated.
- Make the process of simple choices simple, not difficult
- Help other people make their choices
- Seek assistance without giving up your role of making your decisions

The challenge of choice is all about choosing and then making the results of that choice the very best for you, the group, the business, your friends, and the rest of the world.

One of the key elements in overcoming choice challenges is to recognize how and where you make choices. We all have choices every day and they range from very simple to very complex. Whatever the choice is, something has to be accomplished. Not making a choice is a choice.

Random — the coin flip, the `she loves me, she loves me not', whatever first pops into your process. Random works for simple choice — restaurant menu, TV program, stop at next gas station when fuel tank is near empty. For complex choice, random is rarely effective.

Research — How much time does one spend on research can be based on how much data needs to be collected. You will never gather all the information about any one choice process. You can do a shallow analysis by seeking headlines and basic facts. You can do deep analysis by locating many sources and view content, images, facts and opinions. My view is to do what it takes to be comfortable with your choice. Deciding where to go on vacation is not as complicated as deciding to take your company public.

SALY — the long followed `Same as Last Year' only works when the circumstances are the same. If you enjoyed a vacation spot, you can return. Taking a company public will not be repeated quickly.

Lightning Strikes —Ben Franklin's key and kite discovery can provide some immediate `AHA' moments of inspiration. These moments can be helped if you gather usable information and see how they are connected. Your `AHA' can leap from the content on your desk, whiteboard or computer.

It's a Mystery — sometimes choices are made and no one knows how they actually were done. You can spend days trying to figure it out or move on to what is next on your agenda.

Someone Else — try to avoid having other people make decisions for you. Making choices with another or with a team can work great. Avoid having someone else choose because you made the choice not to be an active participant in the process.

Therefore, when it is your turn to make a choice — '*Do It*'.

Your goal is to make choices within the timeframe that they need to be done. Avoid missing any opportunity to make a choice. We all get better with practice — especially when we **"Choose Wisely."**

Do, Done, Did

- How do you manage your to do?
- Are things getting done?
- Do things stay on your famous list seemingly forever?

The world of "To Do" has to migrate to the stage of "Done" so that you will be able to talk with people about what you did. This is not impossible, but does require your active participation. Just thinking about your To Do list is a start. Thinking should never be the only action.

There are, of course, lots of statements made that identify why the To Do list remains that symbol of being overwhelmed. A few of my favorites are: The list is too long; I never have enough time; I cannot do one more thing.

When overwhelmed is an acceptable goal, overwhelmed will happen. Getting rid of the "over" and sticking with just "whelmed" is better.

Getting unstuck from your overwhelming To Do list requires getting started and doing things. It will become a habit when you begin to see results from doing as opposed to making lists. Everything in its place refers to being an active doer rather than a passive list reader.

The Stuck Gap

Part of being stuck lies in the simple reality that we do not know everything. As much as read, as much as we study and as much as we can communicate and learn from others, there is always a gap between what we know and all that there is to be known.

One view is that we possess insufficient wisdom. That is part of the glass half-full, half-empty view. Over a lifetime, we learn a large amount of information - useful, usable, trivial, nonsensical, or fun. All of this learning gets inserted somewhere in the synapses and connections of our memory. Recall is optional.

There will always be a gap between what we know and what we do not know. This underlies why I call an electrician when the repair task is more than fix a plug, reset a circuit breaker or change a light bulb. What you do not know about getting that job, making a decision to move or figuring out how to describe your goals is your STUCK GAP.

This gap could be insufficient wisdom. It could be insufficient money. It could be that you are indeed in quicksand and have not yet found the help you need to get out of that mud hole. To bridge that gap is your purpose. Some gaps are too wide and will not be crossed. Other gaps will give you a choice of which bridge do you want to go over and how fast do you want to get to the other side.

Not all gaps are meant to be traversed. I have not won the lottery. I will not be a professional football player. I will not win an academy award, starring in a movie would have to come first and I am not looking for the location of that bridge.

Learn more. Learn more every day. Make sure that some of that learning activity will assist with your ability to find the bridge, cross over the gap and keep moving towards your goal. Stuck happens. What you do when you are stuck is a choice.

Making Decisions

Making decisions is about selecting from a list of choices that best fit your journey at this time where you are:

1. Do I really need to make this decision now?
2. Is this decision moving me along my path?
3. Am I being honest about the way things are right now?
4. Am I acting and performing in my highest self-interest?
5. Is each decision in the best interest of everyone touched by the process?
6. Am I delivering my best shot to what I am doing now?
7. Will I take full responsibility for the outcome, no matter what that outcome is?
8. Do I understand the real significance of this action?
9. Have I reached out for valuable assistance?
10. Do I answer all of the above questions in a way that makes me feel good?

◆If you answer "NO" to any of the above questions, keep seeking better answers.

◆If all answers are "YES" then you are making decisions your intuition agrees with.

Never hesitate to ask for help.

Going Somewhere

The study of where we are going can provide interesting and/or perplexing results. We can go to the left, we can go to the right (please, no politics here). Sometimes obstructions make the decision for our going. Sometimes, we just turn on a whim. Sometimes we stop and stay stuck to whatever we are standing on.

Here are a few suggestions:

- Now is the time to get going, answers do not walk up to your front door

- Find joy where you go and tell stories about who you are, not who you were

- Doing tops planning

One who lacks the courage to start is already finished.

Go ahead - your start button is waiting.

Richard Oppenheim

I guide people to exit from the powerful grip of indecision and self-doubt by generating a personal map to navigate the road ahead.

I Help You to – *Make* **Decisions,** *Get* **Past Roadblocks,** *Take* **Action and** *Pursue* **Positive Results. Getting more done will lead you to more – net revenue, job offers, connections, work / life balance.**

Losing sight of your path is a time for action to engage my GPS Navigation Experience to help you engage accountability in everything you do.

Other Print and E-Books

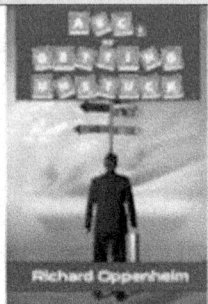

Print and eBook versions available through Amazon»
Amazon Author Page- http://amzn.to/oGPLOi

richard@gpsfyl.com

Web / Blog   www.gpsfyl.com

www.linkedin.com/in/richardoppenheim
www.facebook.com/richard.oppenheim

Find Your Place

Navigate Your Journey